The Adventures of
Dofesaba II 2018

"From West to East via the Canals Du Midi"

PETER J. BELL

AuthorHouse™ UK
1663 Liberty Drive
Bloomington, IN 47403 USA
www.authorhouse.co.uk
Phone: 0800 047 8203 (Domestic TFN)
+44 1908 723714 (International)

Because of the dynamic nature of the Internet, any web addresses or links contained in this book may have changed since publication and may no longer be valid. The views expressed in this work are solely those of the author and do not necessarily reflect the views of the publisher, and the publisher hereby disclaims any responsibility for them.

Any people depicted in stock imagery provided by Getty Images are models, and such images are being used for illustrative purposes only.
Certain stock imagery © Getty Images.

All images in this book and all text is the property of the author, except those images from Google Earth – which contain the Google Earth registered trade mark

This book is printed on acid-free paper.

ISBN: 978-1-7283-5277-0 (sc)
ISBN: 978-1-7283-5276-3 (e)

Print information available on the last page.

Published by AuthorHouse 05/12/2020

author HOUSE®

Contents

Dedication

To Mary, mother of my four children, my partner in life, my crew on the boat, my life friend. My wife.

Foreword by Nigel Campling - Chairman of the Southerly Owners Association

Peter and I share several interests, one of them being the joy of owning and travelling in a swing keel sail boat. We are currently (2020) both circumnavigating Spain, he clockwise and me anti-clockwise, and we will undoubtedly meet up in a bar somewhere *en route*.

What follows is a fascinating insight into the trials and tribulations of moving a 42 foot sailboat, without its sails, eastwards across France in the height of the Summer. The text is self-deprecating, part travelogue, part Pilot and part yarn and is told in Peter's mildly irreverent style.

Peter amplifies the tale with his knowledge of matters historical, which brings to life some of the places visited; as does many of the lovely photographs he has used.

I hope his words will encourage you to explore this wonderful area and the engineering marvel that are 'The Canals du Midi'.

Nigel Campling
Chairman – Southerly Owners Association
Owner – Dutch Courage of Cowes (Southerly 115)

Preface : by the author

This book, albeit the first to be published, is one of five in progress. I started writing up our adventures after my work dried up with the shrinking of the Oil Exploration business in May 2015. I then found that I had time on my hands and that we could 'go sailing' for longer than the two weeks that we had been constrained to, by being in work. As a Consultant Geophysicist, if I did not work I did not get paid; so longer than two weeks was 'undesirable'. As of 2015 I was *free* (but poorer) so I decided to document our adventures more accurately and more definitively. I also felt in 2015 that as I was now a mature 61 years old, that soon I would not be able to 'adventure' quite so much, and one day I might have grandchildren (even though this is not my decision – thankfully) and wouldn't it be nice for them to read about what Grandad & Grandma had been doing all those years ago. It was also at this time I started researching more of my family's history and finding out the part my Grandfather had played in the Battle of Jutland and the very narrow escape he had. (There is a book in there somewhere which I have not yet written; who knows.) and also finding out from my father about our suppressed Scottish heritage, which to be fair had always bugged me (My name is Bell, it is written on whisky bottles from a firm in Glasgow – why did no-one mention Scottishness to me) Then with underemployment I had time, I also felt that I was capable of telling an entertaining tale. I hope you will agree with this statement after reading this book.

So many different reasons for writing these books of which this is the most unusual from a 'sailing' point of view, in that there is absolutely no sailing, even though our boat, Dofesaba II is a sailing yacht. As you will find out within the text. It/She is a Southerly 42 ft Sailing yacht. Not to put too fine a point on it, she is a special boat in that she has a lifting keel powered by an electrically driven hydraulic system, and this enables a large sailing yacht with a 2.7 metre draft to go through the Canals of France, which have a 'minimum' depth of 1.2 metre – guaranteed. As you will find out, this is French for "we would like this to be true but er... it might not be" and we found it wasn't. Fortunately, our minimum depth with the keel fully lifted was 0.8m – however this was still not shallow enough. To find out why – read on and enjoy.

Acknowledgement

I would like to acknowledge my wife and family without who's support none of our adventures or the writing up of them would have been possible.

Glossary of terms used in Order of Appearance

(For an alphabetical list see back of book)

Bed and Breakfast – like a mini hotel where you stay over night for what is says in the name.

Erewego song – an old fashioned football chant whose lines are

"erewego erewego erewego;
erewego erewego erewego-oh;
erewego erewego erewego,
"erewego-oh ereweeegoooo" – repeat ad infinitum or until all are tired.

Gorn – Cockney for "Gone"

Vittles– Sailor/Pirate slang for Food & Drink, used by sailors in Nelson's Navy – that which is needed to keep one full of Vitality, or indeed "alive".

RLymYC – The Royal Lymington Yacht Club, our local yacht club, close to where we live. Full of adventurous Seniors, several Olympic sailors and us.

The mark one eyeball – a sailors expression for trusting what you see by looking about, as opposed to what is marked on the chart or the chart plotter. Doesn't work in thick fog.

Oenophile – someone who likes wine er... like me.

Holy Moly – a light expression of surprise, acceptable to maiden aunts.

Snifter – 1930's P.G. Woodhousian slang for a "Refreshing Beverage" – most normally a beer.

Summat – Devon/Hampshire/anywhere agricultural in England, for "Something"

Savoie – Region of France close to the Alps/Swiss border. Contains many ski resorts.

Wee Snoozy – Scottish slang for a Siesta or a rest in the afternoon, not necessarily due to a long and convivial lunch.

VNF – *Voie Navigation Francais*- the body that runs ALL the French inland waterways

Moolah – American slang for Money

Pootle – A verb to go forward whimsically, slowly, and without purpose or rush.

Booze – British slang for any alcoholic drink.

Transom – the back end of a sailing boat

"Lor' Luvva Duck" – Cockney expression of surprise (I have no idea why the Lord would not like ducks in the first place)

Condom – an alternative word for a male prophylactic

Les Bleus – nickname given to the French national football team – as in "Allez les Bleus" or "Come on the Blues"

Trundle - A verb to go forward steadily, not fast and not erratically. More purposeful than "pootle"

Beer o'clock – a moveable time, when one decides to have one's first beer of the evening.

Restos – short form of Restaurant.

Fustercluck – English expression derived from the American, which is just as meaningful and onomatopoeic, yet does not aggrieve anyone, particularly maiden aunts.

AGM Batts – Absorbed Glass Mat - a different, more modern and efficient type of Lead-Acid battery.

TSR2 – a British designed fighter bomber of the late '50s 'pulled' by Harold Wilson as too expensive. Only 1 ever flew.

The Aerotrain – French designed train that ran on a single rail suspended by air pressure, cost a fortune. There is still a 60km test track south of Paris. Pulled by Valerie Giscard D'Estang.

Hobbit Hole – part of the boat that allows access to the engine, heating systems, water pump etc. Chief Engineer Mike's least favourite place – as he spends a lot of time down there. It is under the saloon seating, and can get very warm.

Zut Alors – French exclamation. Used a lot in school French books of the '60s and '70's for teaching French

Nowt – Yorkshire/Northern for "Nothing" (opposite of 'summat')

Woah – Exclamation of surprise, often accompanied by throwing one's hands/arms into the air

Bulldog Drummond – British adventurer of the Empire. He never gave up and was "British" to the end.

Jack Hawkins – Screen actor particularly in British war films where he played tough, emotionless, never-say-die war heroes, however he sometimes did. (Die that is)

Bimini – Canvas shelter on the back of the boat that connects with the sprayhood to give shelter from the sun to the whole cockpit. Allows you to steer a boat without being burned in thirty five degree heat.

Holding tank – an internal tank for keeping human waste until you reach a pump out facility.

Mr Sulu - a Star Trek helmsman of the USS Enterprise.

Plonker – East end (of London) expression for an idiot, twit etc. often used as a noun for the male penis, which to be fair is not known to have a lot of sensitivity or sense.

Bow Thruster - an electrically driven fan within the bow under the waterline that swings the bow (Sharp end) left or right. Almost all Southerlys have them – particularly those with twin rudders as it is impossible to steer a large vessel without one when travelling at under 1.5 knots particularly going backwards – as in when berthing. Many have a stern thruster too, allowing sideways berthing – but we do not, preferring to use our finely honed skill set.

Le Boat - is a French company that hires out cruisers to anyone who will pay the price –no boating competence is necessary and rarely visible. It is not the only boat hire company, but it is the largest and has the worst reputation.

Push pit – The railings at the back of a boat that stop you going overboard backwards. Usually made of bent stainless steel tubing. The pulpit is the same thing at the sharp end. In the film "Titanic" Rose put her arms out where I keep my pulpit – it doesn't quite have the same dramatic effect when Mary tries it on Dofesaba II.

Blatter – A verb somewhere between "Blither", "rattle" and "Chatter" To talk enthusiastically about a subject, often without noticing that no-one is listening. Often seen at parties after two glasses.

Splot – An Australian verb for putting sun cream on your body

To T Bone – as in another boat, to hit them in the side creating two right angles either side of your prow / Sharp End. If two fibre glass boats hit, the sharp end of one is flattened and it creates a hole in the side of the other. If either are made of stronger stuff (Wood/Steel/Concrete) then a more obvious disaster can occur. A manoeuvre to be avoided at all costs. Sinking is often the aftermath.

Towing Bridle – a method of connecting a rope to a sailing yacht so that the pulling force is evenly distributed to port & starboard, and the vessel can be towed straight (ish)

Hammerhead - the top of the T at the end of the pontoon, usually reserved for longer boats or catamarans, so called because the map of the pontoon looks like a hammerhead shark, or even a hammer.

Hivernage – Literally "Wintering" the boat is lifted out of the water and stored on land, on props so it is safe, until needed next sailing season – or May 2019

Introduction

We had wanted to take our Southerly 42 RST through the Canals du Midi (Incorporating the Canal lateral de la Garonne, the Canal du Midi and the Canal de la Robine) for several years; it was one of the reasons why a Southerly was the boat for us. We had been planning it for three years, and succeeded in getting the boat from Lymington to Royan in 2017, which was an adventure in itself. (see "The Adventures of Dofesaba II 2017" – yet to be published – 2020)

We had been unable to convince any friends to accompany us, which was a little disappointing, but that is the way it is.

While in Royan, during March 2018 myself and Michael (chief engineer and boat fixer) had removed the mast and boom, packaged it all up, sent it down on a trailer to Port Leucate and put it into storage, where it awaited our presence at the end of the summer.

Our adventures were delayed by the marriage of son Francis to the lovely Hollie, which was enjoyed by all. Once they had disappeared on their honeymoon – it was off we had to go.

Chapter 1
ARRIVING AT THE BOAT

It had been a long week in Cornwall with Francis and Hollie's wedding and we returned to Lymington with just a few days before we left for France. Oh, and we had to attend another wedding celebration in a pub in London, as parents of the groom but this celebration was for various cousins, and other relatives and friends who were unable to attend the wedding in Cornwall.

Anyway on the Sunday, we awoke in a bed and breakfast just outside Stansted airport and managed to get to the Ryan Air flight in plenty of time. Skipper started to get a bit excited and began singing the 'erewego' song to himself, as a light smile creased his tanned and weather-beaten crinkles. The plane landed in Bordeaux without fuss, then it was onto a train to Royan. At last, we were there, just a short walk off to the port via the main drag. Lo and Behold – no boat. "Gorn" it was.

Dofesaba II getting ready to leave, without mast or anything that projects above the top of the sprayhood

For a moment, panic raised its ugly head before the normal 'Check & check again you silly old fool ' leapt into my forebrain and caused me to steady up. To be honest this has been a maxim that has kept me mostly alive and also saved many a relationship. Mary, Dominic (Our son and the first part of Dofesaba II) and I had turned up at the wrong part of the port (what can I say, there were masts everywhere and one bit of Port Royan looks just like another) After I had realised this and searched the *correct* part of the port, there she was; in all her magnificence – quite lovely, err..but without her mast, wind generators, aerials and so on, so not really that magnificent. Even so we were pleased to see her lovely blue hull & ivory coloured decks.

We continued down the sloping stairway to the pontoons and boarded her. What a filthy vessel we found. There had obviously been some rain with Saharan sand mixed in it, as well as general dirt, as everything was filthy. We ignored this and went for vittles and thence to bed after a long day's travel. Oh! and England scored 6 goals in the World Cup, so quite a memorable day.

The next day was spent making extra preparation for the journey to the entrance to the Canals, which are situated south and east of Bordeaux. We decided not to rush, but to take maybe three days to get to Castets en Dorthe (CeD) which is the entrance lock of the first part of the Canals du Midi, but first we had to get up the Garonne via the Gironde.

The Gironde has a fearsome reputation, but this is where the intrepid crew of Dofesaba II do not fear to tread. So we left Royan after refuelling and checking the tide. It was a beautiful day and nothing could go wrong, apart from pushing one to two knots (kts) of tide for a few hours and nearly hitting a few sand-bars – it didn't.

Dofesaba II tied up in Braye *Halte Nautique*, where the VERY large boats stop

We arrived at Braye after spending an hour at 9.9 kts We also noticed that the tide appeared to lessen and change about 1500 hrs. The *port* of Braye is a *Halte Nautique* or a stopping place to get your breath back when the tide changes. There are many in the area, as sometimes the tide can be greater than five kts either way. Braye is a very small, but historic town, with Roman remains and a seventeenth century Citadel designed by King Louis XIV's favourite fortification designer; Seigneur de Vauban. We stayed the night after ensuring we had a minimum of five separate lines to shore, which was an unusually large amount and once in a while – they were needed. Fortunately, I had heeded many warnings from our friends and fellow RLymYC members, Clive & Tricia, to take more fenders than I thought I needed. So now we ran with five to seven a side depending. (Normally in UK or down the coast of France we would use three to four per side but tides are fiercer here) We were berthed on the outside of a pontoon obviously designed for a big vessel, but *Madame La Capitainerie*, the controller of berthing in the town hall, or *mairie*, said it was ok to stay there, until our departure at midday on the following day, so we felt safe enough to leave the boat there.

On leaving the pontoon to go watch the France-Denmark game in a bar somewhere in Braye, we were inundated by well-meaning mature French and Dutch folk suggesting to us that they had seen a 100 metre vessel parked on our pontoon the other day and we should move. Aren't people nice. We explained that we had checked with the Town Hall that it was OK, and so they all shook their silvery heads and muttering, returned to their camper vans . Dominic and I carried on to a *Bar-Tabac* to watch the world cup football.

Wednesday promised to be over thirty three degrees so we laid in lots of squash and fruit juice as well as little mini snacks to have during the long journey to Bordeaux. My book said the tide would turn about 11:41 – but local knowledge suggested 1400 hrs. Well I couldn't wait that long so at 12:05, off we set.

Leaving Braye - Our track is in blue and the ferry track is in pink.

Braye is an interesting part of the Gironde as it has lots of moveable sandbanks and I had previously watched the ferry leave from the quay next to where we were tied up and seen the path that he had taken to avoid them. Now bear in mind we were on low tide, as that is when the change occurs from downstream to upstream, so when we left, I steered a course based on plotted depths that sort of followed the ferry path yet avoided the highest sandbanks, knowing that we had a minimum of 1.4m of tide above CD. (chart datum) The depth gauge was working well and had been calibrated to the nearest centimetre. So off we went and just as I left, so did the ferry, it was a little unnerving. When it came to the first sandbank (1.4m deep) we sailed across happily and the ferry turned away – but then we went towards the second sandbank and as the depth gauge descended, up came the keel, until we had ten to twenty centimetres of water under the boat (0.9m deep and the keel depth is 0.8m) I could feel the ferry skipper thinking *Zut Alors – 'ow did he do zat*! as we skipped into the deep water channel feeling very smug about being a Southerly owner.

A small diversion on Southerly yachts. - All Southerly yachts built by Northshore Yachts of Itchenor, have a ground plate of cast iron, and a lifting keel, also of cast iron, which is lifted at the touch of a button, using an electric pump that pushes hydraulic fluid into a ram that is connected to the keel by a Dyneema pennant or strop. It takes about thirty seconds from full down to full up and slightly less the other way around. It is very satisfying to do this, particularly if one is stuck in the mud due to tidal miscalculations. This speciality gives lots of confidence, but does add a major factor to the price. Other sailing yachts can have lifting keels, but the mechanism for lowering and raising is nowhere near as clever, easy, neat, or expensive. Hence the smugness of all Southerly owners.

Then it was up to Bordeaux passing *Chateau* after *Chateau* surrounded by aprons of darkish green grape fields. This area is the *Haute-Médoc*, then the *Médoc* and eventually *Graves*, some of the most intensively graped parts of France. Another pleasure of this trip was that it was really pleasant going under bridges knowing that you had oodles of room, no need to duck as the mast scraped the bottom of the bridge, let alone worry about dangly power cables. That did not stop me ducking under the first one though.

Just about to leave from the Pont Henri (or Norge)

So after three hours into the journey (at 1520) the tide turned – contrary to all expectations – but now I knew how it all worked. The tide would turn to go upriver when my tide clock reads half tide falling and changes to downriver at half tide rising. There was a five minute stand. Later that day after pulling into *Ponton Henri* by the *Pont Pierre*, I checked it against the mark one eyeball, which I have often found a little more reliable than some of my instrumentation.

Interestingly the lady at the *mairie*, where we had to register our presence, told me that the landing stage on which we had berthed had been renamed *Ponton Norge* and was not referred to as *Ponton Henri* anymore except on all the maps, guidebooks and charts, I joked that this was to confuse poor English sailors – She did not disagree.

We stayed in Bordeaux for two nights, parked next to the Police and Fire Brigade launches and left the day after England lost to Belgium. That day we went on a tour of the vineyards of the *Médoc* (in other words back up towards all the *Chateaux* that we had passed on the river two days earlier – this was very frustrating) which was some consolation, who would have realised that there were that many bottles of wine. What of a challenge for an oenophile.

This years wine maturing in the cask, prior to bottling and sending to China

As a matter of interest, we still have not seen *any* other (non-commercial) boat going our way.

The next day leaving the *Ponton Norge (or Henri)* was planned for 1230 hrs, a little bit earlier than when I expected the tide would turn, (see above) all crew holding ropes ready to cast off and the engine in neutral – tide still 0.5 kts against us, then I put the engine into forward, about to shout "cast off all" – when there was an almighty *chunga chunga chuncka* noise – "Holy Moly what was that, the gearbox broken? A thrown con rod ? what is happening ?" I panicked not, and disengaged the gearbox. I then selected reverse and the same noise – yet another "Holy Moly", this was really not good. I then leapt off the boat and re-attached all our lines really quickly and tried to explain to the bewildered and apprehensive crew why I had done that, (this was a bit tricky while brain in overdrive, trying desperately to discover *why* the noise had been there) . We were then all tied up nice and safe. I then examined the prop area, to see a subtle tree branch one centimetre in diameter with a few leaves attached had appeared under the transom – but it was not moving. I assumed a small branch had got stuck under there. So I discussed the situation with the crew – I explained that I may have to dive down in my wet suit – seriously not something I want to do as:

1) the water was still cold as it had just come out of the Mountains and it was still May
2) the water was very dirty & brown
3) there were many lumps of solid, sharp vegetation visible, moving at speed.
4) I was terrified,
5) Mary was unkeen.

I decided not to go into the water there and then, and to wait and see what happened when the tide turned. Dominic and I waited for half an hour, all kitted up and all prepared with safety ropes and other equipment, also with one of us hyperventilating in terror (er... that was me) and then just like that, the tide went from one knot that-a-way within five seconds to one knot the other way and all of a sudden this massive tree came out of the back of the boat – no kidding, it was six metres long with loads of branches and a trunk twenty to thirty centimetres thick with some very new white notches in the trunk. So Dom and I wrestled it onto the pontoon so it would not harm anyone else and got away really quickly – and thence to Begles.

By now it was gone 1500 hrs and we arrived at Begles after 1800 hrs – and *Madame la capitaine* that I had spoken to on the phone to book the berth, had left for the day – so we took ourselves off to the nearest resto for a snifter and vittles while the tide screamed around and through the pontoon we had tied up to.

We got to 'Mercis' – a really nice looking place and managed to get a table for three people. Some beers arrived very quickly – which was excellent, followed by a plateful of eighteen oysters .

"But we didn't order any oysters" – says I in a surprised tone, and in French.

"mssr they are free",

"but they make me very ill"

"but this is the whole point of this high class restaurant, we bring you food you cannot eat and you pay us a massive fortune"

To be honest, I then realised we may have made a small error in regard to my selection of restos (not summat I do too often) – We extricated ourselves and went to the bar down the road, and there had a nice meal & a few beers and saved a fortune. I don't think I was designed to be French.

our route from Royan to the start of the Canal de Garonne

Chapter 2
ARRIVING AT THE CANAL ENTRANCE

The next day we set off for the canal entrance at Castets en Dorthe, but first a fond goodbye to Dominic who had to return to work in Savoie, France to contribute to our pension pot for at least another thirty years, and once he had left for the airport, Mary and I left for the canal entrance.

The first lock into the Canal Lateral de la Garonne. Mary holding tight

We arrived at Castets-en-Dorthe one hour too early, according to the lock keeper. So we had to hang around until lunch had been taken, but after that, we were allowed into the canal – at last; after so many years thinking & planning – how strange to be here. The temperature climbed to thirty five degrees and Mary was not too happy – so we stopped at the marina there and relaxed. Thinking to ourselves – 'no pressure, we can take ages if we want to', so a wee snoozy was required before continuing our adventure.

The next day it was off to Fontets – this promised a bathing pool and lots of free wifi – huzzah!. We arrived there and had a swim in their campsite pool. The 'bathing pool' is a bit of a pond with imported sand dumped on the edge, but at least it was not canal water – but in thirty six degrees, it was still welcome. We decided not to connect into the wifi and just relax as all that connection malarkey could be left until the following day.

That night a massive storm crossed our area and while no harm was done to us or the boat, the *Grande Orage* or in English – 'Massive Thunderstorm', fried all the Government and marina owned wifi systems (and some of the non-govt. systems too I expect) such that wifi is unavailable for three days, and as I had just run out of data on my phone – 'tings were getting desperate, as we were going to meet Brian & Elizabeth in two days time at a place yet to be finalised.

Small diversion – Brian and Elizabeth we have known for twenty years, they do cycling holidays and this year Elizabeth had organised a bike ride for them both, starting from Sette (far east of the Canal du Midi) to Saint Malo (where they were due to catch the ferry to England) via the Canals du Midi. We only found this out late last year when we visited them, and so the inevitable "why don't we meet up somewhere then" said I, after a few of Brian's beers, and so it was organised. Damazan was originally supposed to be the meeting place – but I needed to change this to Buzet sur Baise, hence the urgent need for comms.

We left Fontets at 1000 hrs in plenty of time to get to Mas Agenais (on the way to Buzet) All was well with the world. I woke up that morning feeling a year older, this being explained by it being my birthday- I was 64 – I have always said I am *very* happy growing older as the only viable alternative was considerably worse. The lovely Mary brought me a nice cup of birthday tea and then we were off. All remained well, pootling happily through a cathedral like arch of mature plane trees while the sun dappled down between them.

The view forward from the cockpit – sometimes you could see fields either side, sometimes the vegetation was too dense, it depended on the VNF maintenance schedule.

No other boaters in sight at all. We went through a few locks handling them like the practiced professionals we were, while I continued steering quietly and ruminating slowly, as you do when the way is straight and there is little to do. When, suddenly an alarm bell went off in my head and I retuned to planet Earth. I looked about, we were not about to hit anything, the canal remained dead straight, we were slap bang in the middle of it and the engine was purring away happily, but hang on, no plashing noise of water exiting the engine. *aaaaaaaaargh* panic! that is not good.

A small diversion on Marine Diesel Engines: we burn diesel – not much, but some – burning hydrocarbons of any description is a standard well known chemical reaction that provides power, generates CO2, and particulates and er...increases the temperature. (Some would argue that this 'destroys the environment', well it doesn't do it any good I'll warrant, but then I am not after a Govt. grant) Water from the canal is sucked up by an impeller linked to the engine, driven around a heat exchanger so as to cool the engine. This was not happening, eventually if this situation is left unsolved, the engine seizes and you cannot go anywhere, (don't forget, we don't have a mast, therefore no sails, therefore no alternative motive power) one is, to put it mildly - stuffed!.

"MARY" I shouted "problem" and moved the boat to the bank. Mary got out the mallet and stakes and I secured the vessel beside the canal. Still absolutely no sign of life or anything except green trees and green water. We then set about trying to solve the problem.

Pulled over to the side, miles from anywhere, solving blockage.

Was it

1) Loose fan belt – possible; easily fixed but not very likely, I checked that, tightened it a little anyway, but obviously not the problem.
2) Broken impeller – unlikely, as I had put a new one in this year – tricky to fix, decided to leave investigating this more fully until last.
3) Water filters – very likely, lots of weed around, easily fixed.

Yet another small diversion – several years ago when the idea of *doing the canals du midi* had occurred to me, and back then when I had sufficient moolah to afford it, I discussed with Michael (the Chief Engineer and general Guru of boats) how to ensure we did not have - weed blockages- as the Canal Lateral de la Garonne on which we were a-pootling was notorious for excessive weed. The solution he came up with was a dual filter system that could be easily accessed from a floor panel and while one filter was working, sucking water, the other could be isolated and be cleaned thereby never having to turn the engine off – sounded damned clever to me and so Michael built and installed it, with some assistance from me I might add. (well, I held his screwdrivers)

Mary and I lifted the floor boards and cleaned the filters, but that was not the problem either.

4)   The input pipe to the filters was blocked – very likely indeed – but VERY difficult to get at and fix.

Now bearing in mind this is now 1300 hrs and it is twenty seven degrees outside (and a lot hotter in a small cramped space while working with screwdrivers) and the sweat is pouring off me, my shirt is soaked and I am 'down there' working in the bowels of the boat trying to wrestle with recalcitrant fittings and I am not strong enough, or my hands are too slippery to remove the necessary hose from the skin fitting, I am feeling - stumped. Mary suggests that it would be better if I took a small rest, a drink and lunch, and that I did a little more thinking before any more 'doing'. I realised that sometimes she displays tremendous wisdom. Reluctantly I agree that she has a fair point, thereby displaying a very small amount of wisdom myself, not much but just enough. A thirst quenching light beer and a sandwich later, my brain starts to work. I recall the great Tom Cunliffe had a similar problem with a plastic bag over his engine inlet and he blew it out with a foot pump (as used on inflatable dinghies) I didn't have a foot pump, but I did have a very strong electric pump. Several minutes later, we had connected it all up, the leads to the twelve volt sockets were just long enough and with the pump balanced on the stairs, and with Mary looking out for bubbles I turned it on.

"Do you see anything" I called from down below.

"No" was the reply – I looked out to see Mary with her head looking out over the transom. I explained that anything to see would be where the intake was, which was one third of the way along the starboard side and would she please look there instead. (To be fair I had not specified that earlier). So we tried it again.

"Anything"

"oh yes, lots of turbulence but no bubbles" hmmm, that was puzzling, I closed the stop cock removed the air hose and opened the stop cock again and just avoided a face full of water from the pressure of our depth, which made me very happy on many counts.

"Huzzah!" I shouted "it is clear". Now all we had to do was to reconnect everything, retighten all the things I had undone and be on our way. Our log says we restarted at 14:45, exactly two hours after stopping. It had to happen on my birthday, so I sang a lusty chorus of "When I'm 64" and pottered off to the next lock. We arrived at Mas Agenais at 1800 hrs, way after everyone had gone home. Even the church had shut.

Mas Agenais is famous in the guidebooks for its Church (11th Century) its Rembrandt (within the church) and being the place where the Venus de Milo was found. (in a nearby Roman villa) The following morning I got up and visited the church to find a large space on the wall illuminated by a spotlight, but *no* Rembrandt. After translating the French, it appears that the communité could not stump up the cash to keep it in the tradition it deserved, nor with sufficient security to ensure it was not nicked. The upshot was that the local bishop had it transferred to his Cathedral in Bordeaux, so he would not have to travel so far to view it, leaving a large blank space for the good burghers of Mas Agenais to contemplate. It was a very nice old church, very Norman, but it lacked a certain *je ne sais pas*.

Then it was off to Buzet (I **had** to stop there for a beer) but first I had to fix the foreheads as visitors might use it. (we have a certain great respect for a clean lavatory in our house. Nowt to do with me – I am a man – this explains it, I am told) This particular maintenance project took a little longer than expected and so we were an hour late meeting Brian & Elizabeth. It was so nice to see them, they stayed the night and left early next day after a lovely dinner and some very nice wine.

Brian & Elizabeth dressed and ready to continue towards St Malo

After our fond farewells, we returned to the boat to start clearing up, when half an hour after Brian and Elizabeth had left, John & Julie arrived. It was lovely to see them too, after their two hours drive to see us. We managed to persuade them to stay on board for the night as opposed to searching the local campsites for a doss-down place in their rather flimsy tent. I deemed this a very wise move as that night, torrential rain, massive thunderstorms and all that accompanies them, descended upon us. I think they were pleased we had made the offer to stay on board.

On the fifth of July, John and Julie carried on north along the canal to Royan and we decided to deviate down the River Baise, which joins the Canal Lateral de Garonne at Buzet by a large double lock. The Baise is a tributary canal of the Garonne. Now I had heard of at least 3 Southerlys that had been along the Canals du Garonne and the Midi, (Gneiss Fantasy, Distant Shores & at least another whose name escapes me – I am 64 you know), but I have never heard of anyone going up (or down) the Baise. Being very Dofesaba II – this did not stop us. After John and Julie left at 1000 hrs we entered the double lock to descend ten metres to the Baise.

The River Baise – under maintained this year, almost totally blocked.

Now being my usual laissez faire self (see how this French gets into everything) I had not gotten the map out (as our American cousins would say) so we progressed gaily (in the old fashioned sense) in the direction of the exit of the lock, ie North. Remember the self checking mechanism we alluded to earlier – well the sun was in the wrong position, and I just felt "wrong" (You try having this feeling in New Zealand – I just felt wrong the whole time I was there – it was very discombobulating I can tell you) but I was in France – Northern hemisphere – I felt I was going the wrong way, and when I checked the chart – I was – Huzzah!! I know what to do, turn the boat around. Unfortunately the boat is twelve and a half metres long and the canal at this point is ten to twelve metres wide. So being a wise skipper – I waited till it got wider. Fortunately this occurred just before the weir which blocked the way up the northern arm of the Baise. I turned her around within a boat length and away we went, ducking under the canopy as we repassed the lock we had just exited.

Lunch was at a pleasant Roman town called Viannes and thence onward upriver towards Nerac past Levardac, and on our way to Condom, which just had to be visited if only for the fridge magnet. While the rain hammered down, we avoided many massive tree roots and other obstacles and eventually I put Mary down on a tiny pontoon at St Crabery (it was two metres long – a small fraction of our boat length (well a sixth to be accurate)) and off we went to get the lock to open, leaving Dofesaba II on this mini pontoon. We then cycled the lock to allow entrance and I returned to the dock and jumped back on board. I cast off and went to enter the lock. All was going well, we were trundling slowly forward at less than one knt when we stopped - dead. *"What"* I exclaimed– we had become stuck in the entrance gate. At this very moment the four ton hydraulically powered lock gates started to close on our fragile glass fibre hull – Mary; very cleverly banged the emergency stop button to prevent the gates trying to close on our fragile hull, while I tried desperately to back out.

A Yanmar 4JHE diesel engine as fitted to a standard Southerly 42 RST can develop 55 HP and with my prop rated for more forward motion than backward, on full power I can do about 45 HP in reverse. So I did. Nothing happened except for lots of noise, judder and swirl out of the back end. Using the bow thruster, I wiggled her from side to side while on full reverse thrusters. Slowly we moved backwards an inch at a time (to be honest I was in France, so it was more like 2.54 cm at a time, but I wasn't focussed enough to go up there with a micrometer) and so after fifteen minutes of this, we suddenly popped out of the lock at about four knots - backwards. Breathing many sighs of relief, I picked Mary up at said pontoon, made the decision to go no further upstream, and went back the way we came. I now fully understood why previous Southerlys had not tried the Canal du Baise. As it was nearing beer o'clock we stopped at Lavardac, a town well loved by the Lord. This was another of those lovely little French villages on top of a hill with an old church, a town square, a single bar and café and very few tourists. We stayed here and had a coffee and a beer, while thanking our lucky stars we had extricated ourselves from yet another potential disaster without damage, except to our pride.

Parked in Lavardac – note the lock and the total lack of facilities – the boat looks nice tho'

The following day it was back to Buzet, and back to the bar with the TV set which by now we knew well and they knew us too. I spent the afternoon and evening being an honorary Frenchman and cheered on Les Bleus, and later on an honorary Belgian cheering on Les Belges (two separate games you understand)

In a bar in Buzet – lots of Booze visible

Chapter 3
BACK ON TRACK

We had to get to Agen the following day so an earlyish start was required, because –

1) there were few stop off points
2) I had to get there by 1600 hrs as the England game started then.

Over the famous Agen viaduct. Underneath is the River Garonne

This was accomplished including the four chained locks that led up to the famous Agen aquaduct taking the canal over the River Garonne, this took us about an hour's hard graft in thirty two degrees and by the time we arrived, we were severely dehydrated and a bit knackered. I only had half an hour to find a bar with a TV. Now this might sound a bit strange but where the port is situated in East Agen there are very few bars and none open, it is also home to the Muslim population of Agen – possibly a link there.

However the *west* part of Agen has a nice selection of bars in a square. I chose one with the least people in it and asked in my best French if the match was on.

"*Mais oui monsieur*", I then proceeded with a conversation – very little of which I fully understood, but I appeared to hold my end up. While singing "God Save the Queen" quietly to myself the patron asked me if I particularly liked *les Anglaises*, to which I replied

"*Bien sur Mssr, parce que je suis Anglais*" (Of course sir as I am English) and with this he flounced off in a bit of a huff. Apparently I had 'deceived' him, by imitating a French man (*Quoi ???*) but after half an hour of grumping behind the bar he saw the funny side of it and after England had scored a glorious first goal, he became my friend. Unfortunately I stayed there a whole beer longer than was necessary, so I was a bit wobbly on my return and did not cover myself with glory. I had over-celebrated. We all make errors – me more than most.

The next day it was Sunday and nothing moved in the town until gone midday. I then spent several hours in the Musée de Beaux Artes surrounded by Roman & medieval artefacts, along with paintings by Dégas, Monet, Sissons, Rembrandts and a lost Tintoretto. You have to ask yourself how did a small town in south west France get all these magnificent (and expensive) works of art. The answer was that apparently nearly all of the exhibits in the museum were donated by successful Agenais over the years so as to embellish their birthplace and give themselves some status in their hometown, even tho' many did not live there. It was an illuminating two hours.

A statue of a Roman goddess made out of Gypsum, illuminated from above. Very mystical.

Then it was off to Valence D'Agen – nice early start, I thought we would stop at Booe, as it has a nice ring to it and our 'Bible' (AKA A Waterways Guide to the French Canals #07,12 & 16) promised a vibrant stop with the ability to change our empty Gaz bottle. We duly arrived there to see a ghost *Halte Nautique*, impossible to land on, as they were repairing the quays and there was just no-one or thing visible, not even a *Capitainerie*. We came to the conclusion that our Bible was not always reliable. We passed the nuclear power station at Golfech (very difficult to miss due to a massive chimney emanating steam to the heavens). Thence to Valence, which has nothing much to recommend it, save the ubiquitous main church. The log says I had an extra beer today when I heard that Boris Johnson had resigned.

The following day it was off to Moissac to meet the Chamberlains. Fortunately, it is a lot cooler today. We arrived in Moissac to meet "Jim" an Americano-Brit who with his girlfriend/life companion runs the *capitainerie*. As expected, he is larger than life and very amiable, we agree that I can leave the boat tied to one of his Quays while we visit our friends. All is well. Peter Chamberlain, AKA Chambers, comes to pick us up at 1930 after we have cleaned the boat up a bit (at last, a chance to clean up – but I did get chastised (by Jim) for using valuable drinking water to make Dofesaba II look better)

A small Diversion: Peter Chamberlain I have known since we were eight, and he and I have been sort of planning this for two years – the "when you go down the canal you really must come and stay with us, in our second home in France as it is not far away from the Canal du Midi" conversation had been had over many years and many beers at different meets. So we did. We made it happen. Mary loved it, a bed that didn't move, a cool pool, solid ground, all the things women love. I thought it was lovely too, as I had someone to drink a beer with me. Peter and Dulce took us to some fine restos and some lovely medieval towns, not easily accessible by canal, and allowed me to watch the football in their living room. What a friend. During this period, there weren't any dramas at all, very little to say except book reading, pool splashing, wine drinking and food eating. During our stay the temperature levelled at about thirty five degrees most days, so having the pool there was a godsend.

All this easy life could not last forever. I dragged Mary back to real life on the boat and at 1040 hrs on the fifteenth we set off for Castelsarrasin. Not a big hop, but several chains of locks to get through, as well as another aqueduct over the River Tarn (which is apparently very famous). Unfortunately the middle of the chain of three was not working well, so a delay of twenty minutes while the VNF (*Voie Navigation Francais*) man came out to reset and fix it. We pulled in to the Marina in Castelsarrasin and watched the World Cup final in a square across the road, where the local town had set up several beer points and a very large flat screen. In the blazing sunshine I joined many 'loud yet joyous' French folk to watch their national team beat Croatia, and thereby win the World Cup.

A small portion of the crowd watching the World Cup Final in Castelsarrassin – all ages but mostly youngsters, lots of beer and lots of local police 'hanging about' – keeping control. Just in case.

They did not stop the celebratory noise until one to two a.m. and many cars passed the moorings 'a-hootin' & a beepin' all night long'. As nearly all the residents in the boats and on the pontoons there were 'not French' we kept our heads down, turned over and sighed. To be fair it was a nice game and the French were worthy winners and deserved their celebrations.

We left Castel (as we locals and cognoscenti call it) at 0930 with our state of charge at 66% and we knew we had eight locks to go through; a chain of three then a single, then a chain of four. All the time I was worried about our state of charge as 66% was not so good

A small diversion on batteries : in previous years we had 'made a small mistake' about our batteries believing them to be *Non-Maintenance* or Sealed. This means you can forget all about them for five years, and then it becomes time to change them out, as they are now pretty knackered. With *Full Maintenance* Lead-Acid batteries one needs to check them monthly, top them up neatly and look after them and they last around seven years. They are also cheaper. There is a lot going for them. Unfortunately we had assumed we had put in *Non-Maintenance* batteries and when there was a massive fustercluck in the power department, only then did we realise that they were "please look after us well" batteries. We could not have that happen down the canals. So the year before the trip I ripped the bad ones all out (to be honest we had abused them so badly they would not hold a charge for more than a day or two and were extremely unreliable – therefore worthless) and I replaced them with AGM batteries. These batteries are extremely low maintenance (ie you do not need to touch them) they can go right down to 20% empty without a serious problem (unlike *Non-Maintenance* and *Full Maintenance* where under 50% is starting to hurt) but they are bulky and *very expensive* so unattractive to most cruising folk – however I love them. This does not stop me getting a bit twitchy when I see my SOC (State of Charge) less than 70% as this has been ingrained into my head. End Diversion.

So we get to Montech, which is another very famous place. In 1974 the head of engineering a Mssr Jean Aubert of the Canal de la Garonne had an idea to save some time going through locks; even though people had been using chamber lock technology for 3-400 years – he came up with a scheme to slide a boat in a pool of water big enough to hold it, and bypass all those pesky lock thangs and just slide the boat and the water up (or down) hill. All he had to do was provide a seal so the water did not leak out, and something to provide power to move the several tons of water and boat up (or down) hill.

The Montech Water Slide, the tractor units – now disused, yet a technical monument

So from 1974 to 2009 the powered water slide at Montech all worked and a marvel of French engineering it was too, er.....except 40% of the time it broke down. It cost a fortune to operate (subsidised by the French Govt. of course) and was only available to commercial traffic, which even in 1974 was being surpassed by road and rail. (Holiday makers could use it if they paid €200 and what canal boater is going to do that, most boaters try to get a free night by skipping off in the morning, so saving €10) – anyway it is now derelict, but I was determined to see it as engineering marvels should always be appreciated (eg the TSR2 and the French Aerotrain, both of which I have visited)

Montech marina was ok and we hitched up the power and paid for some more, but that only got the SOC to 70% - I felt summat was not quite right. We departed next day and our power take up was very small, so when we had to wait for a lock I went downstairs, And lo; I was right – *again*. (I am used to this). It turns out the fan belt had loosened itself yet again, I mean it was dangly, not just loose. How did that happen. Out with the spanners, down into the hobbit hole and retighten the bottom nut, up to the top, tighten again the top nut. All this in only twenty six degrees, so, not too bad then. I now felt confident in my fan belt tightening capabilities.

Behold, within three hours pootling we made it to 100% - smiles all round (well Mary & I anyway, there weren't many others all around to share the joy, unfortunately) and so with joyous hearts it was time to find a mooring in a place called Grissoles. Now this was advertised as an official *Halte Nautique*, and when we arrived we found that it was 'under maintenance' but there were spaces for just three boats. Two boats were there already with *just* enough room to squeeze me into the back bit. Well obviously I managed it, but not without frightening the chap in front when I waved my rather large anchor ten centimetres from his superstructure. He intimated to me that he felt this was a "bit too close" and while I insisted no harm had come to either boat, I DID agree it was a "bit too close".

Grissoles, the following day, similar to many other Naturel Moorings

Grisolles was a 'Naturel Mooring'. This means that you can park there, but we are not going to assist you in any way, for instance, by providing nice sturdy posts to tie to, or a nice flat landing stage for your wife to step onto, *non! zut alors!*, you get a bit of river bank and sort yourself out.

In all the guidebooks to the Canals, you are encouraged to take with you on board a large club hammer and some metal or wooden stakes, which give your boat the reason to stay where you left it. The fact that there may be nettles, thistles and small nasty bitey critters on said bank is nowt to do with it. However it is very cheap – now you see the advantage for many folk.

The following day we left Grissoles and carried on and "Woah" – met another boat going the other way. Now this may not sound too exciting for you – but we had spent many days on the canal pootling along, not seeing anybody going our way, or even the opposite way. Being a considerate member of the RlymYC (Royal Lymington Yacht Club) where we are encouraged to be polite to ALL boaters no matter how incompetent they may be, I moved right over to the starboard side as he was hogging the deeper middle ground. He waved cheerfully as he forced me to ground very close to the starboard bank. "Bastard" I grimaced in French quietly to myself as we slowly came to a halt, stuck to the bank sides. After some cool manoeuvring we were off and running, BUT the engine did not sound right at all, could it be blocked again ???– oh yes it was – so back to the bank, tie up on the stakes – but this time we knew what to do and working together we had blown out the blocked pipe and were on our way again in under half an hour. What a team! It was so nice to know what to do and have us both working towards a common goal. I was really pleased with us, particularly Mary (I am used to me knowing what to do) and so on we went to Lazarisse.

This was another 'Naturel Mooring' advertised as being 'just before the Lock' but when we got there, there was very little to distinguish it from any other bit of river bank, so we just parked. As I was manoeuvring to this prime berth the port rudder grounded hard into the mud of the shallow bank and we stopped. Fortunately this was exactly where we should have been, so I shrugged my shoulders in a gallic manner and tied up fast. I was sure summat would turn up. I got the beers out and sat down to contemplate the universe with Mary, and looking over my shoulder saw an immense black cloud. Sheltering my beer under the canopy for obvious reasons, we sat and watched the giants throw rocks at each other/the angels have a dispute/static discharges within the local atmosphere churn air masses so as to amalgamate water particles (delete as appropriate for your religion) and so it thundered, lightninged and rained. And did it. Within one hour we had floated off the mud, almost as if any prayers that should have been said, had been said.

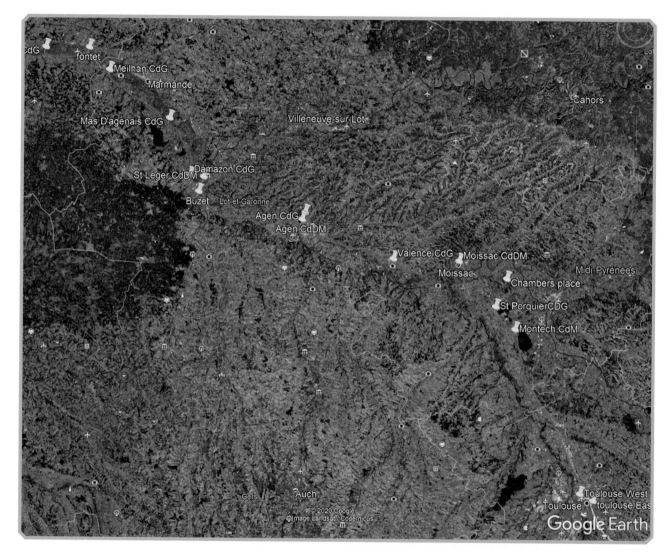

Our Route Casterts en Dorthe to Toulouse – end of the Canal de la Garonne

Chapter 4
ENTERING TOULOUSE, THE END OF THE CANAL LATERAL DE LA GARONNE

The next day it was off to Toulouse. As we got ever nearer it became obvious, we were getting closer to a bigger city. The number of P and R camps increased, (P and R really stands for "Poor & Ragged" and is shorthand for homeless people) the graffiti on the walls multiplied, the number of dead/ very unloved boats parked on the side, increased and so did the traffic noise.

Entering the Centre of Toulouse

However we were booked into *Port St Saveur* in the heart of Toulouse, so we could sight-see and just rest up. Little did I know. We exited the Canal du Garonne and then we had a little hug and congratulated ourselves on finishing one canal; but we were not over the hill yet. So we turned straight into the Canal du Midi and proceeded through the town to the first lock. We arrived at 12:10 – which as we all know, means that it is French Lunchtime, so nothing works, at least not until 1300 hrs. After getting all excited we 'stood by' until 1300 hrs. We then entered the first lock of a chain of 3 – this means you cannot stop until you exit the third lock as *Mssr Ecluse* (The Lockkeeper) is watching on his camera and cycling the locks as you go ahead. So we didn't, and we ended up safely in *Port St Saveur* albeit later than expected, and because I had phoned earlier, they had assigned us a prime berth, right next to the office and the on-foot exit to Toulouse. What we did not know was that the berth chosen for us was not an easy one to get into. *Madame Capitainerie* asked me if it would be a problem for me, as we could have another berth if we felt we could not get in.

This was a bit like a red rag to a bull, so I stiffened my upper lip, in a Bulldog Drummond/Jack Hawkins manner (as In the Cruel Sea) then prepared the crew and went for it. We glided in perfectly and stopped before hitting anything and within a few seconds all tied up. By now we had garnered an audience, they all clapped – which to be fair was well justified, but very different from normal behaviour. I wish that happened every time we tied up, I feel it does, but only in my head, it rarely does in real life.

Toulouse was neat – some super monasteries and churches to review as well as museums, all interspersed with cafes and bars for refreshment purposes as usual. Abundant *supermarches* and the *Marina St Saveur* was really nice and the staff very helpful. So much so, that I decided to fill up with fuel. This required me to move to the diesel pontoon; but I decided to transfer fuel from our jerrys into the main tank and then fill the jerrys from the pump, much easier than moving the boat. We had been motoring for quite a while, so the tank was sure to need topping up.

In *Port St Saveur* just about to top up the tanks – the two red cans are 20 litres. and the small black can is 10 litres.

The first twenty litres went in fine, but half way through the second twenty litres there seemed to be a bit of a blockage but I got it all in eventually. I was very pleased that unusually I had not spilled a drop of Diesel onto the superstructure of Dofesaba II around the entrance to the tank as I had carefully laid tissue paper all around to catch any drips, of which there were very few.

Several hours later my boat neighbour came around and asked if I had spilled some fuel, as the other end of the marina stank of it. I informed him that while I had filled my tank, I had not spilled a drop – very pleased with myself was I. We then both looked out the back of Dofesaba II to see a film of diesel trickling down the transom onto the step and slowly into the water. While I had been pouring diesel into the tank situated amidships, it had all leaked out of the overflow and poured discreetly into the canal for about an hour.

Oh! the abject humiliation! what a massive plonker oi be. I then spent three hours trying to clean it all up with wodges of paper towels and washing up liquid and any other dispersant I could lay my hands on. The local fire brigade were called and came and had a look, but by the time they arrived, I had cleaned most of it up. The *pompiers* all walked around, checked, shrugged their gallic shoulders and went back to their coffee. I was not Mr Popular that night – but endless apologising in French assuaged the wrath of all. Nobody invited me for a beer during our whole stay. The following day I was having a beer (by myself) on the back deck as the sun went down, when I spotted a critter in the water, swimming in a carefree manner around the basin. Soon all the boat people were watching it. Was it a beaver – the two Americans thought it must be, but the tail was rounded not flat. Was it a capybara – that would be tricky as they live in South America. It turned out to be a *Ragondin*, which I had never heard of. This translated to 'European Coypu' which to be honest I had never heard of either. Anyway for the next two nights he popped up at around dusk and watched me drink a beer. Weird critter.

We left Toulouse in the morning, and it was off to Montgissard, through several locks as ever. We parked on the bank *au Naturel* and left the following morning towards Gardouch where again we stopped *au naturel* beside a lock with a very nice bar/resto. The following day was more important, as we went through the lock called 'Ocean'. This is the last lock where we were going uphill, from now on it was all downhill to the sea. You would think this means it would be easier and to a small degree it was – but not by much, as we shall see later. That night we moored by Segala lock, where I cycled off to the monument to Paul Ricquet situated on the highest point of the whole canal complex. Without his genius none of this would have been possible. I was all alone in the blazing sunshine so I murmured a word or two of thanks and cycled back to the boat. Regarding the sunshine, we had been happily pootling along in twenty four to twenty eight degrees for the last couple of days, which is pretty hot even under the sprayhood and bimini, but this day registered thirty four degrees for four hours. It was the start of some uncomfortable cruising.

The monument to Pierre-Paul Ricquet between the Locks Ocean and
Mediterranee and slightly off the canal by about a kilometre.

We left Segala early as we had 8 locks to go through to get to Castelnaudry, our first double followed by our first triple and several singles after that, all in downhill mode which we had not tried before. It took a while, and in the heat, Mary was not too comfortable – but we did it.

Castelnaudry is the home of *cassoulet*. This is a local dish which is very famous. As ever, I had never heard of it. It consists of a duck leg, some chunks of pork sausage and white beans in a stew. Now we had had some of this before and it was not really to my taste. During our exploration of Castelnaudry, we came across the Castelnaudry museum,

"This has got to be worth a look to see the local history". Said I to myself.

No such luck, it was all about how you make *cassoulet,* including pictures of ducks (hopefully long cooked) and of fields of beans and even a video on a loop of a very old women making *cassoulet* in the 1950's. I felt quite cheated of my entrance fee of two Euros. Anyway that night we decided to order a special *cassoulet* from an advertised local firm. The "we will bring it to your boat, after being cooked locally by some very old peasant women" version. To be fair it was scrumptious. Maybe those who had provided the previous versions had not seen the video.

Then it was on to Bram. This DID have a museum all about Bram, and Romans and medieval street plans and Counts and bishops etc, not a bloody word about *Cassoulet*. I really enjoyed it. A fascinating place. Then it was on to Carcassone – for me the highlight of the trip, a town I had been dying to visit for many a long year, and that deserves a new paragraph, if not a new chapter.

Toulouse to Carcassone

Chapter 5
GOING DOWNHILL VIA CARCASSONE

Carcassone is a medieval fortress, and during the 12th-13th Cent. was the home of the Cathars. Unlike many castles in England and also France, it has not been "updated" since the 14th cent. So it remains in a state different to that which we in England and Europe are used to. Louis the 14th of France upgraded many castles in France for the advent of siege cannon and he asked Vauban to do this, and so almost every French fortress near the coast and inland has been adjusted in Vauban's distinctive style; mainly as a defence against English naval attack. Carcassone, being a long way from the coast, was not considered worth the effort, so it remains a very special example of pre 17th cent castle building. I urge you to visit it. We stayed five days and thoroughly enjoyed it all. Unfortunately the castle itself had been 'desecrated' (My opinion) with a work of modern French art.

An aspect of the curtain wall at Carcassone with a piece of modern "art" imposed on its ancient, yet hallowed walls.

from the special vantage point it
all sort of makes sense.

This involved painting yellow circles all over the battlements & towers so that when viewed from one particular spot (and only one mind) one could see lots of symmetrical yellow circles. From anywhere else in the whole valley, particularly the town and river area below the castle, it looked like vandalism on a grand scale. As one can imagine, queuing to stand on the one spot where it all made sense was a bit of a scrum, but all was made possible, as it always is.

The castle had also been vandalised in the 1960's and 70's, but this time by the French Archaeology Dept. The *Directeur* had not only cleaned up the ruin, but decided that the turrets (which had mostly fallen down) needed rebuilding. As there wasn't a plan of what it really looked like in the 14th Cent, he decided to give each of the 13 turrets a different cap. So several look Roman, at least 3 look like they were from the Rhine in the 1600.s Several are direct copies from the Chateaux of the Loire (18th – 19th Century) and one or two put there much later, to try to give a flavour of the 13th Century. In all it looked a bit of a mess, but do not let that put you off a major visit.

Berthed as we were in the marina, we were next to Wolfgang & Virginia, two very respectable and very well dressed Berliner pensioners, who at every opportunity when they returned to their boat insisted on removing their clothes. They tried hard to be discreet, but when the wind blew, down came their protective screen, revealing a pair of naked pensioners, it was hard not to notice. This did not manage to put me off my cool beer tho'. Here we also met Frederick, a pleasant Swiss from Basle who very nicely asked us to accompany him to other places away from the canal, including the most incredible Cathar stronghold on top of a hill called Montsegur. We viewed it from the bar below as it was a 500 metre climb and in thirty five degrees at the time. Try to imagine what it would be like to be a Royal Infantry man told by the General Inquisitor to "go attack that castle", "Yes that one, the one on that humungous hill, full of people trying to kill you"

If you get a chance, go visit Carcassonne as it is well worth it, but it does not need me to say more than "we visited it" in a chapter on the Canals du Midi.

The mountain fastness of the Cathars, Montsegur

The next stop (*au naturel*, yet not as *au naturel* as our Berliner friends) was to Marseillette, another tiny village with its own Radio Station, and very little else of note. Then on to Homps which is a slightly bigger town/village (two good restaurants, one of which came highly recommended by Brian & Elizabeth, so we had to try it) It was very jolly indeed, so jolly that we had to sit under a tree and just admire the view. Our log records that we had five days of thirty eight degrees and this stop was right in the middle of it and might explain why we stayed there so long.

Sitting under a tree admiring the view (with a cold beer) in thirty eight degrees

Another Small diversion : I may have mentioned that, several years ago we had put in several extras onto the boat in case we ever did the Canals, and one of these extras was six Caframo fans. These move the hot air about swiftly while cooling the body, but only to a certain degree. During our early sailing years in the Aegean we had been stuck in small cabins in sharp ends of boats in early 30.s temperatures and found it impossible to sleep or even live. Hence the need for these fans. However thirty eight degrees from lunchtime to about eight o'clock at night, then slowly decreasing to thirty five at bedtime made life very uncomfortable for Mary, so much so, that we worried that she may be getting heat stroke, as she showed mild symptoms of it. At least with the fans on full power, we could sleep as they are very quiet and they did move the air about, but obviously not as effective as any kind of Air Conditioning. I don't want anyone to get too excited, but I didn't wear my woolly pyjamas for several weeks due to the heat. We became a bit sluggish and very unmotivated to move on quickly even though our original intentions for the trip were 'to take our time'. The unforeseen benefits were that whenever I needed a cold beer, I was able to blame the excessive heat. Mary cooled herself by soaking a T shirt and a neck scarf in coolish fresh water and wearing that until it dried, then she repeated the process until bed time. It is not often I spend time with Mrs Wet T shirt. When we were in the Aegean there was always the option to dive over the side of the boat and cool off. This is not recommended in the Canal du Midi or its tributaries. When you get there, you'll see why.

1) All of the places that suggest in the book that they have pump out facilities – just don't, or if they do, they haven't worked for quite a while. We never used one.
2) All the fellow canallers on hire vessels we talked to, told us they did not have holding tanks on their hire boats and their waste went straight into the canal.

Hence the need for as much cooling on board as is possible.

We left Homps hoping to reach Somail, but we were stymied by *madame L'eclusier* (Lady Lock keeper) who decided to go to lunch early and stay out late just as we arrived at her lock, which unlike many locks in this part of the Canal du Midi had very few reasons to stay there. To be fair this was very unusual as all the *Eclusiers* (lock keepers) we met except this one, were very pleasant and very helpful. Eventually we got through the lock, but by that time the temperature was up to thirty eight degrees and Mary started feeling poorly again and had to lie down. I got the boat to the next convenient point, a place called Paraza, and tied up to my stakes, again a green mooring. Much later when it cooled down a bit, I walked into the town and found nothing. No shops no bars – nowt. Just nice houses, oh and an Art Gallery. Apparently, it is what every tiny French village needs. However it was shut when I was walking about – and I was all alone I might add.

The following morning we upped stakes and went off to Somail, but as we got there so quickly as it wasn't far away, we decided to press on and stop somewhere else. Onward we pootled until we came around a ninety degree bend to find a massive dredging barge hiding EXACTLY around the corner where I could not see it . I had a "full reverse thrusters Mr Sulu" moment, and managed to avoid clobbering several tons of steel with my eggshell plastic hull. I don't think the workman on board was too bothered. A gallic shrug and a *petite* wave later and we had passed him safely with approximately ten centimetres to spare either side.

A small café with enough room to moor – but closed.
The secret swimming pool is under the aqueduct in the right background

More pootling and we came to a small café that was, as ever, totally closed but had a nice mooring point exactly thirteen metres long. An ideal place for a lunch stop, and while it looked closed from where I was, by the time I got there I was sure it would open to provide a beer and some vittles. So we glided effortlessly into the mooring and tied up. Still no life, so we prepared lunch. As had to happen, as soon as we sit down, a character arrives to open up the café.

"You cannot park there, that space is for customers"

"Well I would have been a customer if you had been open"

"Well I am not open until four o clock" (It was midday)

"Well can I stay here til then"

"Only if you buy something,"

"That sounds fair to me, I would love to, how about a cold beer"

"Argh we are not open to sell beer until four o'clock"

"Why don't I stay here until five o'clock and you sell me a cold beer at four o'clock"

At this point a lot of thinking went on and ponderment crossed his craggy visage. "Okay" he says and disappears into the building. Now all of this happened in French so I may not have got the translation perfect – but we left the boat there and went off and returned at four o'clock and stayed til five o'clock and had several cold beers. I do feel sometimes that the power of logic is a dying art.

During the intervening time we walked down the tow path and found a night berth in Port La Robine and also the secret swimming pool under the aqueduct. This is where the Canal du Midi crosses the River Cesse. That's right, as in 'pool' so an appropriate place to have one. Bearing in mind the temperature was up in the mid 30's again, this place was full of people 'bathing' in the river that had descended from the Black Mountains so was deliciously cool. The maximum depth was waist high so very safe for children. There were several families making stone dams to make their own private 'wallowing' pools too. I was unable to resist helping a father who was struggling against the flow of the water to bridge the hole made by a small child, hopefully one of his, but we made it after half an hours work. It took me back to my own childhood on the sands at Joss Bay where I learned the art of dam making the hard way. I was thinking of naming it 'The Mohne' when the very small sensitive part of me kicked in and just in case he may be part German, I didn't. (Also I didn't know the names of any French dams, mainly because 617 squadron didn't try to destroy them eighty years ago). After several hours spent exploring in cool pools, we returned to the paragraph above and afterwards moved the boat to Port Robine.

The next day loomed bright and promising, but we didn't have a mast, so we motored down-canal to Capestang, a very lovely village of 2500 inhabitants, but with an enormous collegiate church and some 15th Century ruins of the Archbishop of Narbonne's palace. We parked right outside the *Capitainerie* and squeezed into a 15m space with panache and the judicious use of our bow thruster. Just after we tied up, the boat to our rear pulled out, leaving what would have been a thirty metre hole only 5 mins earlier – thereby making it a lot easier to get in. Having tied up our boat, we left to go down Quay to a nice restaurant/bar and got the table on the outside, so that I had a very acute view of the rear of Dofesaba II. Just as our first beer arrived, we saw a large Le Boat cruising up and down obviously looking for a mooring. I turned to Mary.

"I bet he is going to get in behind us, he should be ok as he has fore and aft thrusters and there are 4 couples on board – more than enough for safe handling"

I returned to my beer, and then the food arrived. Just as the first mouthful was going down I saw the vessel come full tilt into the hole behind Dofesaba II and watched in horror as he rammed our transom. I know that because Dofesaba II tilted upwards forward, and then settled back on her lines. Dropping my beer onto the table ensuring minimal spillage I raced up to see what was going on.

A very large boat pivoting on my starboard transom having smashed already into my port transom. No South Africans were damaged with this unorthodox manoeuvre

To say they were surprised to see a wildly bearded chap enquiring as to what the hell they were doing is an understatement. It appeared they had picked up the boat two hours earlier and had not been told what to do and consequently did not have a clue. Full power forwards vs full power backwards was the order of the day as three chaps tried to keep their vessel disconnected from mine.

In doing so the large Le Boat pivoted on the starboard transom and ended up facing the other way. I managed to persuade the 'Skipper' to leave everything alone and we would manhandle his craft into the space provided, which we did. I tied it all up nicely and advised them to make phone calls and have a nice cup of tea to calm down, while I went to finish my luncheon. It turned out that my life raft casing was smashed and the push pit (or *Balcon* in French) on which it was hung was well and truly bent.

the aftermath of an unnecessary collision. But no one was hurt

Looking down the 160 metre. Malpas tunnel with unfaced pick work apparent (17th century). The other end is all beautifully bricked (18th Century)

I returned later to find four very apologetic retired South African couples starting their first ever holiday in France, so a bit of a downer really. Fortunately they had a form for me to sign which enable replacements and repairs before the next season, but we had to continue knowing that if we sank in 1.2m of water, the life raft would not save us. We managed to live with this.

We stayed two nights in Capestang and did not see the South Africans again even when we left early. We had to do this so as to be through the Malpas tunnel and then to arrive at the Fonseranes staircase by 1300 hrs which is when 'direction down' is scheduled to use the staircase. The guidebooks are quite good on these two points but other canal users are not. According to some, the Malpas tunnel was "really long and dark and you had to walk your boat through lying on the coach-roof" and the Fonseranes staircase "was nine locks one after the other and every one pushes in so as to get into the first lock – first; it's a fustercluck so be careful". Mary and I would nod sagely at these tales and assure the speaker we would be careful and prepared for anything, which we always try to be anyway. What we didn't mention is that we rarely believe these sorts of dire warnings as we have been so disappointed before. Dangerous rip tides screaming through narrow gaps between teeth like rocks in Brittany and the Channel Islands are mitigated by arriving around slack water and sailing through in peace. Vast Brittany style tidal ranges where the possibility of drying out on a rock are circumnavigated by being sure of your position and where you are anchoring, so we take these 'Sailors Tales'" with a bit of 'old Salt'.

We gently progressed towards the Malpas tunnel seeing no other boats, and passed into it and through it admiring the marks of pick axes over 350 years old. No-one had to lie down and no-one got in our way through the whole 160 metres and so it was on to Fonseranes. So far this day had been pleasant, with temperatures in the mid 20's and while there was sunshine we also had a stretch where the plane trees were on both sides, forming a lovely green tunnel, with sunshine dappling through the branches and making the water look very green. (so not due to all the algae, mud, crud, leaves, branches, reeds and poo then, just dappling)

A small diversion on plane trees in the canal du Midi : During the 18th century it was very fashionable to plant Plane trees (See all the parks and squares in London, Paris and other European cities) because they had a reputation of cleaning the air and removing 'dark humours'. Before that the canal had been planted with other types of tree that were supposed to grow to protect the barges from the wind and secondarily to be sold to provide cash for the Crown. After the French Revolution, these were all cut down and eventually the Canal was replanted with Plane trees. Unfortunately, like British Ash trees, these French Plane trees are dying from a fungus (Canker Stain or ceratocystis fimbriata platani) introduced to France in American wooden ammunition boxes during 1944. The affect of this, is that large parts of the canals are treeless on both sides. Thereby losing the protection against the wind and the sun, yet allowing one to experience the life of pre late 18th century canal living. This can be a sorry sight when approaching a stand of trees as usually the first one is dead, the next three are in a gradually increasing health but not looking good and then a burst of normal healthy tress until that stand runs out and the last three are dying with several really dead ones after that. The VNF are gradually cutting down the dead ones and replanting with new trees with an added resistant gene to the fungus. However it is slow and expensive work as these mature Plane trees are enormous and weigh tons. The work can only be done in the autumn and spring, so not much time at all.

A set of dead plane trees. They are fully mature and weigh tons. Their roots extend into the canal

The VNF is the *Voies Navigable de France*, the government organisation responsible for the whole canal system, dredging, trees, water and particularly the locks.

We arrived at the top of the Fonseranes staircase a bit early, so we parked and went for a beer. Looking over the hillside from the patio of the local Café, the cathedral at Beziers dominated the far hill. That was our destination tonight, but first we had to get there. In the queue for the lock it seemed we were fourth in line. There was a chance we could get into the first lock once the direction changed.

Looking down the Fonseranes staircase. It is actually quite a steep climb/descent.

Come 1300 hrs we were on board and ready to slip lines and by that time there were another 8-10 boats behind us. As soon as the last 'direction up' boat was out of the topmost lock and the red *Feu* or traffic light went to green. At this signal, we all cast off and I mean all. All 14-16 boats left the bank to get ready to enter the lock. Being British I awaited my turn to be ushered into the lock, but we were judged to be a bit big for the space available, so I very nicely gestured to the vessel behind me (which was quite small) to go ahead and take my place, and then blow me down, but the next one started coming up too. Well I wasn't having that, so I positioned Dofesaba II right in the way, ready to go in when the lock had cycled, thereby blocking any potential in-pushers. Holding station in a light breeze with very little lee way either side or even fore and aft requires a lot of concentration and I had done this at a previous lock but I had a lot more room there, and using the bow thruster a lot, does run the batteries down. Then I kicked myself really hard, because I suddenly remembered I was in a Southerly – how could I forget that, something I had blattered on to all and sundry for eight years, I had even paid extra for the privilege, something my Scottish heritage still kicked against (I have naturally short arms and wear my pockets deep). I checked the depth, one point two metres and then pushed the special button. The keel swung down into the mud and Dofesaba II was going nowhere, anchored firmly - in the way of all. Smiling beautifully, I turned off the engine and sat back and watched all the other boats going this way and that trying to keep station while I didn't move. Rarely have I felt so British.

A small diversion on the nine Locks of Fonseranes : This is now a UNESCO world heritage site and should you be so minded to look this up on t'internet you will notice that it is always stated as the NINE locks of Fonseranes. This had us very confused as we only went through 7, as I said to Mary – only another two to go… oh there's the exit, what happened to the other two. As you can see from the PICTURE Pierre-Paul Ricquet DID build 9 locks because in his day the canal emptied directly into the river, which is to the north of the turn we took to continue along the canal. At that time the river was a working river but it is no longer, but today after lock 7 the way turns right to go to an aqueduct over said river and thence into Bezier.

a board explaining all about the nine locks – but look carefully for yourself.

The other thing that is apparent from the picture is the remnants of another Montech style Water Slide. (see Montech Above) The Fonserane version was the second and last to be built and like the Montech slide, never really worked properly and it was abandoned in 2001. What is interesting to me is that when you visit the UNESCO site, the water slide part is well shielded by trees, and there is no mention of this abject French engineering failure on any of the heritage sites.

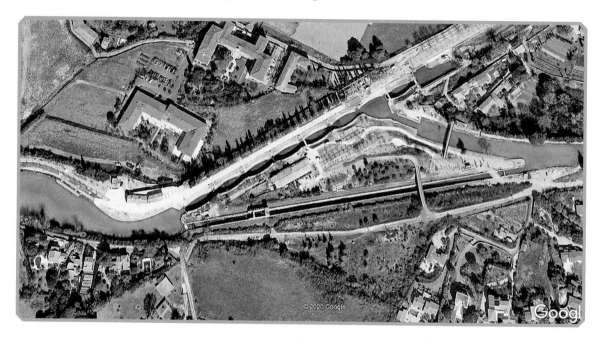

Plan view of the UNESCO site, showing the "almost" nine locks and the alternative water slide that did not work. The top lock is on the left.

We descended the staircase in a controlled manner and made our way to Beziers which is a very beautiful city and very historic. A lovely Cathedral, odd churches, Art Gallery and museum were all thoroughly investigated and enjoyed. (OK also a few bars and Restos) During our stay we visited the Beziers Festival, which appears to be an annual event. We were able to see a Waiter/Waitress race, whereby the winner had to carry a jug of water and four glasses up and down a 200m course and the winner was judged on time and spillage. You can see in the photo that each contestant is accompanied by a minder. This was instigated several years ago to stop the other restaurants 'nobbling' the runners. Apparently it was notorious, and when a young girl got hurt the mayor stepped in and instituted the minder and disqualification. It soon calmed down after that

The Fastest Service person in Beziers 2018

Also on show was the fine old Catalonian tradition of Human Tower building, this must have been a great way to get a village together. We noticed that nowadays the youngsters (usually around five to nine years old depending on size and gender) were all wearing crash helmets. I wonder how many small children got hurt before that was implemented. After that we saw a fine old display of Moorish dancing, complete with grown men in socks, bells on knees, banging sticks and waving hankies. It makes sense really if you think that these dances and costumes came over with the Moors to Spain in the eighth century then up through North Spain, through the gap in the Pyrenees to France (this area was Spanish until the 17th Century) then eventually across the sea to England, being transformed as the tradition travelled north. The Festival was great fun and very colourful, and like everything on the continent, family orientated and very safe, even though there was beer and wine freely available all day and everywhere, a lesson for us all. However after we had stayed a few nights it was soon time to say goodbye to so much enjoyment. It was time to leave for Agde.

Human Tower building – a Catalonian tradition.

Chapter 6
TO THE END OF THE CANAL DU MIDI

Our plan to leave early the next day for Agde was thwarted. Unfortunately, just as we left our mooring turning towards the exit lock of the Marina, a large commercial boat arrived and as they have priority, we let them through. Just as we were lining up for the second opening of the lock, there was a large blast from behind us and a second commercial boat decided it too wanted to go ahead of us. Knowing my good fortune and just the way things worked I sighed quietly when the third vessel appeared. We had only wasted 45 minutes in standby mode, good job we weren't in a hurry. These commercial boats are 40m long and 4.4m wide and literally fill the lock. There is very little room anywhere when they get in. Most are piloted by young French women who are not averse to a cheery wave. They travel in threes and each carries about fifty people with a bar and cool boxes. The engines are very ploddy and they have a single rudder, they are made of sheet steel and they take no prisoners. I stayed out of their way. We eventually progressed to Agde via a lunch stop after which the weather became very hot again. Agde is where the canal meets the River Herault and is a pretty big place with a lovely Cathedral and a museum but otherwise, it was a bit run down. We stayed two nights hoping to meet the representatives of Le Boat to sort out insurance details – but they didn't turn up. Agde is famous for its circular lock, where there are three entrances, or exits depending on your personal philosophy. It is apparently very rare but was not an issue. Once through this, it was off to Sette and the end of the canal.

In the circular lock at Agde. We entered from the left and exited on the right

As we continued, the sides of the canal had fewer and fewer trees. There were few locks and lots of rushes and very open blank bits. The fields had stopped, leaving vast open marsh like spaces where the wind was able to howl across. These are the *Etangs* (or Lagoons) of the Languedoc, which sometimes fill with water and are a haven for birds migrating and nesting in the winter and spring. In the summer when it gets so hot, not too many birds or people are about, and except for a few sailing clubs without club houses, there was very little to see. We exited the canal and entered the final lagoon.

Leaving the trees and civilisation behind, entering the Lagoons of the Languedoc.

By now it was very windy, I have no idea what speed it was but it felt like 25 knts. I could not be sure as our windex (our anemometer) was still on top of the mast in a yard in Port Leucate, where it had been for many months, gathering dust, but it felt 'windy'. For once we had more than two metres. under the keel which was quite exciting. We congratulated each other with a hug and a smile on actually finishing our goal – now all we had to do was to return to Port Robine and go down the Canal de Robine and out to the sea, then reconnect with our mast and boom, drop off the boat and go home, it was all as easy as that, but first we had a lagoon to cross and Sete to visit, just for the fun of it.

from Carcassone to 'almost Sette'

As we ploughed on, leaving the entrance/exit of the canal, life became a lot more uncomfortable and large dark grey clouds were forming on our starboard side (From the sea). The most recent forecast was 40 knots within the hour. The skipper thought it all looked a bit ominous and after some pleading from the crew, made an executive decision to return to the safety of the canal and find the nearest lunch stop, as he was getting dehydrated (again).

Mary looking a lot happier now we have turned around and are heading back into the Canal which starts/ends by the lighthouse. I was happier too.

Unfortunately the nearest lunch stop was quite a distance away but the canal sheltered us a bit until we got to the next lock where we stopped for our own lunch. There wasn't anything about at all. Eventually we arrived back in Agde and parked in the space for the large commercial boats. I felt safe there as I knew they would not be arriving (all three of them) until at least 10:30 the next day. That did not stop many folk reminding me that I would have to move if a commercial vessel arrived. I nodded sagely and assured them that I would. Everyone is an expert on the Canal. We dined again in Agde, but felt a bit underwhelmed.

Departure time was 0930 the next day, our destination was Beziers. The sun was up and a gentle breeze a-blowin, all looked well with the world, time to put some sun cream on body. As I was splotting, we came to a 90 deg bend to the right. I came to the right of the channel and blew my tooter vigorously as I turned – then right in front of me was a large Le Boat with tourists on board, I threw the engine into full reverse at the same time he turned to starboard exposing his whole port side flank almost burying his prow in the far bank. I managed to not T-Bone him by under half a metre and he managed not to swipe me with his stern. I explained in measured tones that he should always try to occupy the starboard side of the channel (not the port side) and that when approaching a blind corner one should reduce speed and blow one's tooter to let oncoming vessels know you are there. A blank expression crossed his rather frightened face, whereupon he said "oh should we, no-one told us that". We both restarted, waved perfunctorily and continued our holidays as the adrenalin was purged from our blood streams, well from mine anyway. It did make me wonder why the hire boat companies did not explain in a little more detail what should be done and the basic rules of the road when they handed over control of a large vessel to an otherwise ignorant human.

Beziers arrived without further incident, a nice big port, stern to moorings this time. I thought we would stay a day as it was very hot and neither of us felt particularly energetic, so a stroll around the port and a snooze after lunch. We would be off in the morning, we had a sort of 'Manana' moment.

We planned to leave at 0900 hrs along with two other boats. Unfortunately they fitted into the lock at the exit of the port and we didn't. Oh well only another 15 minutes to wait. Just as we could see the previous two boats leave the lock in front of us, looking over my shoulder I saw an enormous 40m tourist barge exit from the entrance lock to the port. With a sigh I asked Mary to put the kettle on for another cup of tea as it was surely going to leapfrog us, which it did and sailed gaily into the now opened exit lock. Up it went and out it went, I checked over my shoulder again and a second 40m steel barge with a measly four tourists on board appeared out of the entrance lock. Sipped tea, waited for number two to leave lock, checked my shoulder again to see the expected number three 40m steel barge with two women crew thundering up behind; beside; then in front of me. They entered the lock and up they went. It was now 10:50 and our early departure had once again been severely compromised – good job we weren't in a hurry.

Very soon the lights to the lock went green and we continued uphill to the bottom of the *Neuf Ecluses de Fonseranes*. We knew we had to get there by 11:30 as that is when the 'direction up' set was allowed into the staircase. If you missed this deadline, one had to wait till 1600 hrs. We made it with very little time to spare and had to help a young Austrian couple with a young baby on a small two person holiday Le Boat. They were struggling with the moorings and when we entered the staircase they had difficulty controlling their boat, so Mary very nicely helped them. During our ascent we were very surprised to see hundreds of tourists lining the side of the canal and even getting in the way of the mooring lines. Several pushchairs were up to the edges of the locks, with others pushing from behind trying to get a better look, it became quite dangerous. On one occasion the Austrian couple unwisely handed a line to a tourist onlooker who had absolutely no idea what to do with it and consequently when the lock opened and the water rushed in (the *eclusiers* take no prisoners as they are trying to get rid of you quickly so they can go to lunch at 12:00) and the Austrians' boat bumped into ours causing a small scratch. After the husband had gained control, he apologised profusely and offered to buy me a beer at the top. I could hardly refuse, so we stopped at the café at the top of the staircase for a sandwich and a snifter.

Over lunch we discussed the lack of health and safety exhibited by folk in the marinas and working the canal, particularly as exhibited earlier.

"In my industry, that would not be allowed at all" said the Austrian wife,

"Well that's funny" says I " in my industry we too have very high safety standards"

"oh" she said "who do you work for"

"I'm in Seismic, I look for Oil & Gas and I am/was a Consultant Geophysicist"

"I work for OMV the Austrian National Oil Company and I am a newly qualified Reservoir Engineer" said she.

You, dear reader, have to realise that the Exploration part of the oil industry is very small and most of us all know each other, and I had worked for/with OMV in the past. She had joined OMV after the big crash of 2015 – which is why I had not met her before and she was very young, but what are the chances of that happening – we all sat there flabbergasted.

However lunch was over and it was time to move on to Capestang via the Malpas tunnel, which had been a doddle on the way down. On the way up, we were third in a line of boats and as we approached the tunnel we could see three rowing boats with six people in each of them coming out of the tunnel ahead of us, at that moment the first boat in front of me entered the tunnel and was followed immediately by the second and then by me. I was followed by several boats behind us. As we exited 160 metres. later, all hell seemed to have broken loose. There were about fifteen to twenty crews of six oarsmen rowing boats all trying to get out of the way of the first boat and then obviously all the rest of us too. Boats number one and two were smaller than Dofesaba II and manged to thread their way through the *mêlée* of vessels, some of which were directly across the canal and trying to escape in the confusion, one had even managed to turn themselves completely round facing the wrong way. It seems that we had inadvertently interrupted an annual race and the organisers had forgotten to put someone at our end of the tunnel to stop boats coming through until all the oarsmen had passed. Boat number one had seen a gap after the third crew had exited, blown his horn and entered the tunnel, whereupon all the other rowing crews had come hurtling down the canal and had to come to a dead halt at their end of said tunnel, I do not know the French for 'Fustercluck' but I am sure it was used by many because it was a prime example.

We exited the *mêlée* without damaging anyone's boat but we probably did damage their pride. All I can say is that no-one smiled at us (in French or English) as we went past, even tho' we missed them and waved cheerily.

We stayed the night in Capestang and the next day went to Somail, sailing past Port Robine which is where we intended to divert out of the Canal du Midi. On our way there, we came to a long stretch of canal with no apparent habitation anywhere along the banks and so we felt quite alone, it was getting near to lunch time and becoming very hot. When out of the blue (or even amongst the very young saplings, which are green) was a small board *"Auberge de la Croissade 200 m."* Well *Auberge* means 'Inn' and 'Inn' means vittles – a quick discussion, "let's stop for lunch" and so we park a hundred metres downriver of the *Auberge*. Being the only vessel for miles around and a complete lack of other people should have warned me, but we jumped off the boat, tied it up to our stakes and hove off to said *Auberge*, which appeared quite empty. We were met by a charming Frenchman who admired our French and sat us down on the only table not booked. To my right was a Car Park for many cars and a track leading into the forest, not a road, a track. All of these should have rung the odd alarm bell in my Scottish head but it was so hot and the beer he brought so lovely and his charm was so elegant that I settled down. Then he brought the menu.

A deserted part of the canal – not far from the Auberge de la Croissade

It seemed that we had happened across one of the best restaurants in the Languedoc (well that's what it said inside the menu) and the chef was the well-known mssr top-chef-of-France and they had 2 Michelin stars. It was the sort of place that families took their wealthy Aunt to for a 'nice lunch' *en famille*, as within half an hour the place was packed with very wealthy looking aunts and their families. The car park was full of expensive vehicles (Including Dofesaba II – which was just across the towpath) and there was the rattle of expensive jewellery accompanying the gurgle of fine wines being poured in small glasses, as well as the schlurp of fine beer in a big glass (er... that was me and only me) We agreed that we might as well stay now and hang the expense – so we did. It was of course really lovely, but €85 for two light lunches is more than I can afford every day. After a wee snoozie we continued to Somail.

Somail is quite charming with an antique bookshop that is enormous and very well known. We picked up more reading material and left the next morning to turn down into the Canal de la Robine towards Narbonne, and the sea. On the way, we tried to visit the Narbonne Roman pottery museum but it was closed. So no lunch there then. As we descended the last lock into Narbonne; which was quite deep (2.5m) somehow the line I was looking after on the stern became trapped, I could not free it and all the time the water was going down, the line was stretching and creaking and soon the boat began to creak too and my part of it stopped descending (The rest of the vessel carried on tho') Never have I been so grateful that I always carry a knife and with a single touch the rope exploded and the side bounced down into the water with a healthy splash – that was what we call 'a close one'.

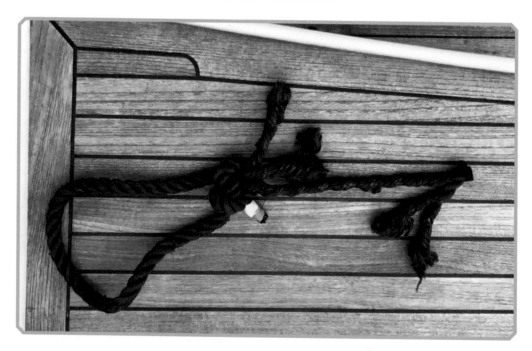

An excessive 1m of mooring line – no longer required. Look at the stretch on it though.

Chapter 7
FROM NARBONNE TO THE SEA

We tied up in Narbonne and spent 3 days there exploring the museums, churches and interesting buildings, particularly the Roman remains of what was once a very important regional hub. On the third day we saw many local chaps in *Cite de Narbonne gillets jaune* building stages and rigging expensive sound and lighting equipment, generally preparing for a fiesta. At this moment the friendly *Capitain* warned us that in twenty four hours our mooring would be full of drunken youth and the music would be playing all night 'quite loudly'. We decided to leave the next morning full of excitement as this was a nice easy run down to Port La Nouvelle and our first taste of salt water in two an a half months. We could claim that we had finished and it was just a short hop from Port La Nouvelle to our eventual berth in Port Leucate; by sea.

In the centre of Narbonne, before the preparations for the Fiesta

Oh the folly of expectation, will we never learn. We left Narbonne at 0935 hrs with blue skies, sun shining and birds chirping. As we left Narbonne, the depth decreased from 1.2 metres to a steady 1.0 metres. This was not too bad we thought; bearing in mind that our draught was 0.8 metres, so we had a whole twenty centimetres under the boat. As we left the second to final lock we were now at the level of the lagoons of the Languedoc which we could see either side, as long as we stood up high on the deck and looked over the canal sides. About 100m after the last lock, the depth descended to 0.9 metres and massive amounts of weed appeared in front of us. I shouted to Mary "I think the intake might block again" as the depth descended to 0.8 metres and a slight grungey noise came from the area of the rudders. At that moment the intake became blocked. With a sigh we prepared to unblock it in the manner we had practised. Then along came another boat with a young French family on board a hire boat. As we were stuck in the middle of the canal he had to manoeuvre carefully and saw that we were in trouble and offered to pull us to the next (and last) lock. I gratefully accepted and set up a bridle and we tried it. At first, all was well, we moved off at 1.0 knts and then gradually got slower.

"I am sorry mssr, but my engine is overheating you are just too heavy"

So I thanked him, disconnected the bridle and let him go and so Mary and I were left in the middle of the canal again with no engine, surrounded by weedy water. We had lunch, then set to with a will. We cleared the engine intake, and decided to lighten ship so as to not get too close to the bottom, we dumped all our waste – emptied the water tanks, moved the spare jerries to the front (to encourage the back end to elevate) and tried to continue.

The depth became 0.7 the speed reduced to 0.5 knts, the grinding noise of rudders going through mud and gravel increased, and we progressed in the same way a snail does. Eventually the speed became 0.1 knts and I decided that summat had to be done, as we were now trapped. I could see bundles of weed around both rudders and I reckoned if I could lose them, we could at least progress. It was now gone two o'clock and thirty three degrees in a windless marsh, I was not looking forward to leaping into the water but it had to be done.

Clearing the weed from the rudders – not a lot of depth here

After I had cleared two man-sized bundles of weed from the rudders, and gone up to shower off on the Transom, did I mention that we had emptied the water tanks. Oh well – onward. We managed 1.0 knot in 0.7m of water for another half an hour and just as the weed cleared, there in front of us was the last lock of the canal – oh joyous sight, and it was open ready for us.

We entered gratefully and Mary got off to cycle the lock, but the exit gate would not open. Would you believe it, one miserable lock gate between us and the sea. We called up for the Engineer who spoke no English and asked me to do something to the gate, in French. Unfortunately, neither Mary nor I had heard the expression he used – so there was some befuddlement. Fortunately a young man arrived. I tried to explain what the engineer had said, and smiling to himself he walked over to the gate and gave it a mighty expression with his boot. Slowly the gate opened and we were free.

"It happens all the time Mssr" he said.

'Well why don't they fix it then' I thought while smiling my thanks in his direction.

Illegally berthed on an emergency hammerhead in Port La Nouvelle

Ten minutes later we were in the sea port of Port La Nouvelle. This is the tenth most important port in the list of Ports de France, so a pretty major place. We found the marina opposite the main fishing fleet dock and came to rest on a hammerhead, as there were no other berths big enough for us. We tied up and got the celebratory Prosecco out, when who should pull up to my transom but The Customs Men (actually they were all women and all carried weaponry). As ever with all French *Douanier* I have ever met, and it has been a few, they were polite and friendly. They checked us over, were surprised we had come from Royan, made sure we had no immigrants, signed our papers and zoomed off back to their mother ship the other side of the harbour. I think they were very surprised to see a red ensign in their port.

Customs mother ship; feared by many, but not us purely innocent sailing folk

We stayed there for two nights while a storm passed through, then set off for Port Leucate which was just an hours run south, where we left the boat on hard storage for *hivernage*.

We were very relieved to have completed our journey and looking back on it, there is a sense of satisfaction of having completed something we had always wanted to do since buying a Southerly 'because we could'. I would not do it again as it is done and there are more sailey challenges that need doing .

You dear reader will be pleased to hear that since 2018, Dofesaba II has been fixed (Rudders patched, scratches sorted, new life raft, new straightened push pit) and in April 2019 we will put the mast back on and she will be a proper boat again, ready to ride the East coast of Spain during 2019.

Look out for the sequel 'Dofesaba II rides again' or less imaginatively 'The Adventures of Dofesaba II – 2019'

Almost Sette to Port Leucate

Statistics for 2018

Total miles this year	410.9
Number of locks negotiated	148
Number of bridges	522
Engine Hours	112.1
Cruising hours	154.2
No of ports visited	34
No of visitors from UK	6 - all overnighters none cruising
No of working crew	2
Time taken	11.5 weeks or 81 days

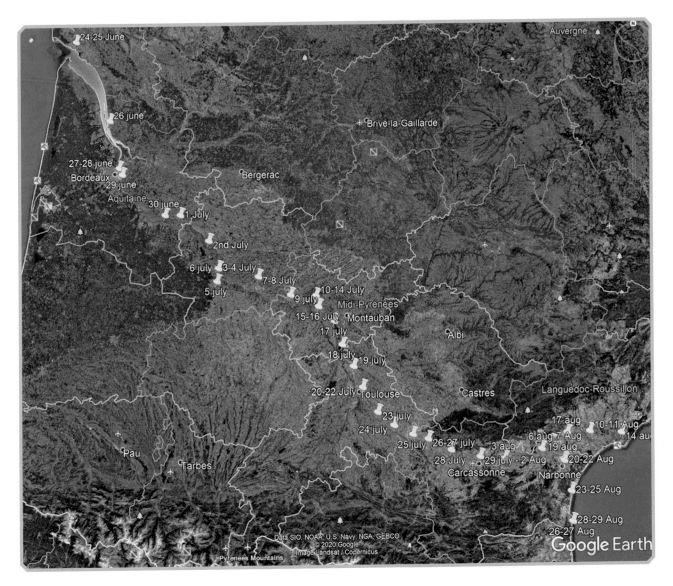

Our route showing all the stops

About the Author

Peter Bell and his wife Mary came to sailing late in the day. Both were Scout Leaders and brought their family up to love the outdoors and to be self sufficient. Peter was a Mountain Leader in Snowdonia until the rules changed and his body stopped working well enough to go up and down. Mary decided he needed a new hobby, on the flat, and so they went cruising on flotillas in Greece. After 3-4 years they bought Dofesaba – a Southerly 110 and two years later upgraded to the S42 RST – in their opinion, the pride of the fleet. In the mean time Peter did Day Skipper, Trans Channel course and Yacht Master Theory exams. Since then, up to 2020 they have 'Cruised' over 9000 miles, with many Adventures. Like many mature couples mostly retired they have used their summers 'wisely'. However, few have the ability to take their boat down the Canals du Midi – so they had to try, and did. This book is the story of their adventures. Peter and Mary live in Lymington and use the RLymYC often. Peter has been known to give lectures on his yearly adventures.

This book in its Log form won the Senior Brownlow Trophy at the RLymYC 2019

Glossary of terms used in Alphabetical order

AGM Batts – Absorbed Glass Mat - a different, more modern and efficient type of Lead-Acid battery.

Bed and Breakfast – like a mini hotel where you stay over night for what is says in the name.

Beer o'clock – a moveable time, when one decides to have one's first beer of the evening.

Bimini – Canvas shelter on the back of the boat that connects with the sprayhood to give shelter from the sun to the whole cockpit. Allows you to drive without being burned in 35 deg heat.

Blatter – A verb somewhere between "Blither", "rattle" and "Chatter" To talk enthusiastically about a subject, often without noticing that no-one is listening. Often seen at parties after two glasses.

Booze – British slang for any alcoholic drink.

Bulldog Drummond – British adventurer of the Empire. He never gave up and was "British" to the end

Bow Thruster - an electrically driven fan within the bow under the waterline that swings the bow (Sharp end) left or right. Almost all Southerlys have them – particularly those with twin rudders as it is impossible to steer a large vessel without one when travelling at under 1.5 knots particularly going backwards – as in when berthing. Many have a stern thruster too, allowing sideways berthing – but we do not, preferring to use our finely honed skill set.

Condom – an alternative word for male prophylactic

Erewego song – an old fashioned football chant whose lines are

"erewego erewego erewego;

erewego erewego erewego-oh;

"erewego erewego erewego,

"erewego-oh ereweeegoooo" – repeat ad infinitum or until all are tired.

Fustercluck – English expression derived from the American, which is just as meaningful and onomatopoeic, yet does not aggrieve anyone, particularly maiden aunts.

Gorn – Cockney for "Gone"

Hammerhead - the top of the T at the end of the pontoon, usually reserved for longer boats or catamarans, so called because the map of the pontoon looks like a hammerhead shark, or even a hammer

Hivernage – Literally "Wintering", the boat is lifted out of the water and stored until needed next sailing season.

Hobbit Hole – part of the boat that allows access to the engine, heating systems, water pump etc. Chief Engineer Mike's least favourite place – as he spends a lot of time down there. It is under the saloon seating, and can get very warm.

Holding tank – an internal tank for keeping human waste until you reach a pump out facility.

Holy Moly – a light expression of surprise, acceptable to maiden aunts

Jack Hawkins – Screen actor particularly in British war films where he played tough, emotionless, never say die war heroes, however he sometimes did. (die that is)

Le Boat - is a French company that hires out cruisers to anyone who will pay the price - no boating competence is necessary and rarely visible. It is not the only company, but is the largest and has the worst reputation.

Les Bleus – nickname given to the French national football team – as in "Allez les Bleus" or "Come on the blues"

Lor' Luvva Duck – Cockney expression of surprise (I have no idea why)

Moolah – American slang for Money

Mr Sulu - helmsman of the USS Enterprise in Star Trek

Nowt – Yorkshire/Northern for "Nothing"

Oenophile – someone who likes wine er… like me.

Plonker – East end (of London) expression for an idiot, twit etc. often used as a noun for the male reproductive organ, which to be fair is not known to have a lot of sensitivity or sense.

Pootle – A verb to go forward whimsically. Slowly, without purpose or rush.

Push pit – The railings at the back of a boat that stop you going overboard backwards. Usually made of bent stainless steel tubing. The pulpit is the same thing at the sharp end - in "Titanic" Rose put her arms out where I keep my pulpit – it doesn't quite have the same dramatic effect when Mary tries it on Dofesaba II.

Resto – short form of Restaurant.

RLymYC – The Royal Lymington Yacht Club, our local yacht club, close to where we live. Full of adventurous Seniors and several Olympic sailors, and us.

Savoie – Region of France close to the Alps/swiss border. Contains many ski resorts

Snifter – 1930's P.G. Woodhousian slang for a "Refreshing Beverage" – most normally a beer.

Summat – Devon/Hampshire/anywhere agricultural in England, for "Something"

Splot – An Australian verb for putting sun cream on your body

To T-Bone – as in another boat, to hit them in the side creating 2 right angles either side of your prow / Sharp End. If two fibre glass boats hit, the sharp end of one is flattened and it creates a hole in the side of the other. If either are made of stronger stuff (Wood/Steel/Concrete) then a more obvious disaster can occur. A manoeuvre to be avoided at all costs.

The mark one eyeball – a sailors expression for trusting what you see by looking about, as opposed to what is marked on the chart or the chart plotter. Doesn't work in thick fog.

The Aerotrain – French designed train that ran on a single rail suspended by air pressure, cost a fortune. There is still a 60km test track south of Paris. Pulled by Valerie Giscard D'Estang.

Transom – the back side of a sailing boat

TSR2 – a British designed fighter bomber of the late '50s "pulled" by Harold Wilson as too expensive. Only 1 ever flew.

Trundle - A verb to go forward steadily, not fast and not erratically. More purposeful than "pootle"

Towing Bridle – a method of connecting a rope to a sailing yacht so that the pulling force is evenly distributed to port & starboard, and the vessel can be towed straight (ish)

Vittles– Sailor/Pirate slang for Food & Drink, used by sailors in Nelson's Navy – that which is needed to keep one full of Vitality, or indeed "alive".

VNF – *Voie Navigation Francais*- the body that runs ALL the French inland waterways

Wee Snoozy – Scottish slang for a Siesta or rest in the afternoon, not necessarily due to a long and convivial lunch.

Woah – Exclamation of surprise, often accompanied by throwing one's hands/arms into the air

Zut Alors – French exclamation. Used a lot in School books of the '60s and '70's teaching French

Printed in the United States
By Bookmasters